Little

Handbook

The
Little Englander's
Handbook

A Xenophobic Guide to Europe and Johnny Foreigner

Major Oswald Kitchener (ret'd)

Edited by David Brown

Michael O'Mara Books Limited

First published in 2001 by
Michael O'Mara Books Limited
9 Lion Yard, Tremadoc Road
London SW4 7NQ

Copyright © Michael O'Mara Books Limited 2001

A CIP catalogue record for this book is available from the
British Library

ISBN 1-85479-553-8

1 3 5 7 9 10 8 6 4 2

Designed and typeset by
SX Composing DTP, Rayleigh, Essex
Printed and bound by
Cox & Wyman Ltd, Reading, Berks

Contents

Few people can be happy unless they hate some other person, nation or creed.

Bertrand Russell

Abroad is unutterably bloody and foreigners are fiends.

Nancy Mitford

So little, England. Little music. Little art. Timid. Tasteful. Nice.

Alan Bennett

Foreword

by Brigadier H. de St C. ('Bunty') Arbuthnot,
CB, CIE, DSO, MC

The late and very great Gerard Hoffman
('Hoffnung') began his famous address to the
Oxford Union with the words, 'When I was
approached by the management of this cinema . . .'
I was powerfully reminded of this when Major
Kitchener asked me to provide a Foreword for
this little book. As I recall, we were in the Snug of
The Average Auditor[1] at the time, enjoying a
swift sharpener before heading back to our
respective bases for a bite of supper.

Few things can beat a fine summer's evening
in Camberley, in my view. Here we were at the

---

[1] Formerly The Wearied Traveller, a title it had held for more
than three hundred years, this ancient inn was renamed in 1997
after it had been bought by the Average Pub Company, a chain
which has turned many fine old pubs into quasi-restaurants
(among others, The Average Accountant, The Average Actuary,
The Average Advocate, and The Average Attorney), providing
television (usually football games) and other entertainments, the
latter invariably involving music played at high volume. The

end of the day, two old soldiers, supping our drinks and chatting desultorily, in the manner of old soldiers the world over. Then I happened to remark that I'd been reading a book. Oswald suddenly became animated, not something one sees often, unless he's hurling abuse at someone.

'That's it!' he cried. 'Book! Knew there was something I had to tell you, Arbuthneg –' for some reason I have never been able to fathom, he always calls me 'Arbuthnegative' – 'been plaguing me for days . . .'

'What is it, then?'

'Written a book. Need you to write a Foreword for it. You know the sort of thing: "Known Major K. since God was a boy . . . splendid subject,

new owners proceeded to gut the building, replacing the two bars with a single giant room 'themed' to represent their designer's conception of a Connemara threshing barn, *c.* 1904. The Snug was to have been taken out altogether, but spirited local protest, spearheaded by Major Kitchener and Brigadier Arbuthnot, forced the pub's new owners to reconsider. It may be that the Brigadier's quoting of Belloc's lines – 'But when you have lost your Inns drown your empty selves, for you will have lost the last of England' – convinced them of the error of their ways. Equally, the appearance of the Major at the company's head office with a Bren gun and a haversackful of charged magazines may also have had something to do with their decision to leave the Snug *in situ*.

exceptionally well handled . . . important matter of grave public concern . . . drowning in bureaucracy . . . precious British institutions in decline . . . ancient traditions slighted or abandoned . . . royal family traduced by gutter press. Etcetera etcetera". Sort of thing you can get any senior Tory politician to do for a fiver, no questions asked. Thing is, though, I know you're not famous or anything, but at least a few people have heard of you, which is more than you can say of most senior Tory politicians . . .'

I thought about this for a moment.

'No,' I said.

'What?'

'No. Not my sort of thing. No can do. Sorry, and all that.'

This was clearly not the answer Oswald had expected. His manner became decidedly frosty, and he began to whine, in the manner of bullies the world over.

'Now look here, Arbuthneg, that's not like you, to let a chap down. Dammit, what would you do if I refused to lend you the hedge trimmer?'

'Use shears. And *not* trim your hedge, for once. Prob'ly take me half the time . . .'

Well, you could tell Oswald was upset, slice it

which way you will, although I'm shot if I know why. After all, I'm not a writer, and don't want to be one – ghastly fellers, all corduroy and funny drinks and slightly too-loud voices. Even the women. *Especially* the women . . . End result is, I can't for the life of me think why anyone would want me to write a lawnmower manual, let alone a Foreword for *A Whatd'yacallit Guide to Europe and Johnny Foreigner*. On top of that, I don't, in any case, share Oswald's view of foreigners. Truth is, I rather like 'abroad', and I've served with enough soldiers from the armies of other countries to have a considerable respect for each and any of 'em – however differently they may do things.

Not that the old boy dislikes foreigners as *people*. He just hates things not to be British. And he reserves his greatest contempt for anything emanating from the EC that interferes with what he sees as the traditional British way of life. Well, no one would deny that there's been some pretty loopy edicts and suggestions from over Brussels way, so to any readers of like mind, I heartily commend this little book.

Brigadier 'Bunty' Arbuthnot, late Indian Army
Camberley, October 2001

Author's Introduction

(*a*) the rusians are roters.
(*b*) americans are swankpots.
(*c*) the french are slack.
(*d*) the germans are unspeakable.
(*e*) the rest are as bad if not worse than the above.
(*f*) the british are brave noble super cheers cheers cheers.

Geoffrey Willans and Ronald Searle, *Down With Skool!* (1953)

So wrote that great English prep-school philosopher and deep thinker Nigel Molesworth, and what was good enough for overprivileged little blisters – or swots, oiks, cissies, milksops and swankpots, in his parlance – nearly fifty years ago is good enough for me. And it ought to be good enough for you.

It's not, though, is it? Or not for a lot of you, anyway. Offered first prize in life's lottery, and what do you do? Trade it, metaphorically, for a pot of cappuccino at a pavement table and a week in Ibiza. So it's not just the EC bureaucrats we're facing here. It's a shamefaced, hangdog, apologetic, 'nothing-British-can-be-any-good' sort of attitude that seems to have affected a large part of the population. By God, we must be even more demoralized than I thought.

Listen to this: here is a Mr Mitchell Bates, one of the 'strategic planners' (how they do love their military analogies, these business types) at St Luke's advertising agency, banging on about the IKEA 'Chuck Out Your Chintz' television advertising campaign, launched in 1999:

> It wasn't just against Victoriana. It was a whole group of associated ideas. One-nation conservatism. The myth of Little England. John Bull. An obsession with the aristocracy, the monarchy. The chintz aesthetic is determined by upper-middle-class aspirations – people wanting to have a country house, even if they live in a semi.'[2]

This, from a man who has taken the shilling of a

---

[2]In the event, although people bought new stuff, there is little to suggest that they did throw out the chintz.

company whose contribution to human knowledge and happiness has been the sale of mass-produced, assemble-it-yourself furniture equipped with incomprehensible instructions. Worse still, the company's from Sweden, a country noted for foisting the open sandwich, stripped pine, Volvos, and the pop group ABBA upon an unsuspecting and largely innocent world. As for Mr Bates, the late Alan Clark said of Michael Heseltine that he seemed the sort of chap who'd had to buy his own furniture (and Clark would have known – his father did just that). Bates, however, sounds like a man who not only bought his, but 'self-assembled' it . . .

We need to snap out of this worship of all things foreign, and especially all things European, because otherwise we're going to sink beneath a tidal wave of EC bureaucracy and legislation that will make the Norman Conquest look like a minor scuffle in the wet canteen of history.

For the point is this: Brussels can tell us what to do – and does. And if we don't like it, they can make us. Yet most of the people in this country go along with all this, maybe with a rueful shrug and a muttered oath, in the misguided belief that our political masters know what they're doing, and that the EC has this country's best interests at heart. They don't, and it doesn't. And the end result? More and more legislation and regulation, much of it inappropriate, some of it plain daft, and almost all of it damaging to the traditional notion of Britain and the British way of life; the increasing 'Europeanization' of our institutions, laws, industries, even our daily life; and the introduction of a piece of toy money called the Euro, which few people seem to want, and is pretty much worthless anyway, so far as I can tell.

Well, it's all got to stop. Everyone's got to pull their socks up, put their shoulders to the wheel, their backs to the wall. And since I know many of you think I'm a mad old blimp who's a couple of tracer rounds short of a full belt, consider this: I heard on the wireless the other morning some erk from a German car company (and I bet he calls himself an 'executive') talking about the plant for building the new Mini at the old Morris[3] works in Cowley. In a thick accent reminiscent of someone playing the

---

[3]Now, those were *real* motor cars. What sort of Englishman is he who doesn't thrill to the names of some of the great models in Lord Nuffield's mighty marque? Think of the Oxford, the Traveller, the Marina, the 1100, the Ital . . . Point made, I think.

Kommandant in a British POW film, *c*. 1951, he said: 'Ze Mini is a Britisch car, und a Britisch legend.' Well, he got the legend bit right. What he didn't add, however, was that the *profits* from the new Mini will be *German*. Get my drift?

Finally, there's another thing that sticks in my craw, which is being called a 'Little Englander' in the first place. The phrase 'Little Englanders' first appeared in the *Pall Mall Gazette* of 1 August 1895, as an expression to describe people opposed to British imperial policy, and especially to any expansion of the British Empire. It has changed its meaning since then: nowadays most people seem to use it pejoratively of anyone who considers Britain and the British to be best.

Well, I do – think they're best, that is – and I believe every other decent, right-thinking, God-fearing, beef-eating, beer-drinking Englishman (and woman, in which case the beer should be changed for a small gin-and-It) should think the same. Mind you, anyone who seriously thinks I'm opposed to the expansion of the British Empire a) doesn't know me very well; and b) hasn't been paying attention. Just the sort of lax approach that lost us the Empire in the first place, if you ask me.

So there you have it. Three simple objectives:

one, resist Brussels – its waste, its power, its language, and much of its legislation – at every turn; two, set your face against the Europeanization of this country; three, say 'No' to the Euro. Then maybe we'll be 'brave noble super' again.

Not too much to ask, is it?

Oswald Kitchener
Camberley, July 2001

Our Fine Qualities

Many people have realized the fine qualities of us Brits. Here's a selection from some of these splendid people, a good few of them labouring under the disadvantage of not being even remotely British . . .

The world still consists of two clearly divided groups; the English and the foreigners. One group consists of less than 50 million people; the other of 3,950 million people. The latter group does not really count.
  George Mikes (*Hungarian by birth, pronounced his name 'Mikash'. A good egg, though, as frightfully pro all things British.*)

Always remember that you are an Englishman and therefore have drawn first prize in the lottery of life.
  Cecil Rhodes (*Mind you, you wouldn't have got the prize if old Cecil had been doling them out at Speech Day. He'd have kept it for himself . . .*)

Only two ways of doing things – the English and the other. We'll not want the other here. Know your enemy.

'Henry Root' (William Donaldson), Root into Europe

The Englishman hates to reveal himself; in fact it is considered bad manners to talk about oneself.

Kurt von Stutterheim, Those English

Courtesy is not dead – it has merely taken refuge in Great Britain.

Georges Duhamel

. . . I am American bred.

I have seen much to hate here, much to forgive.

But in a world where England is finished and dead,

I do not wish to live.

Alice Duer Miller, The White Cliffs (*Interesting, this. An American poetess, she wrote this long narrative poem in 1940, when the country's prospects*

looked pretty bleak. It became a huge bestseller,
though practically no one's heard of it nowadays)

Britain is the most civilized country in the world
and the British people the most civilized nation.
George Mikes, Über Alles – Germany Explored

The English have an extraordinary ability for
flying into a great calm.

Alexander Woollcott

I used to be puzzled by the curious British
attitude to pleasure, and that tireless, dogged
optimism of theirs that allowed them to attach an
upbeat turn of phrase to the direst inadequacies
– 'well, it makes a change', 'mustn't grumble',
'you could do worse', 'it's not much but it's
cheap and cheerful', 'it was quite nice *really*' –
but gradually I came round to their way of
thinking and my life has never been happier . . .
 . . . One of the charms of the British is that they
have so little idea of their own virtues, and
nowhere is this more true than with their
happiness. You will laugh to hear me say it, but

they are the happiest people on earth. Watch any two Britons in conversation and see how long it is before they smile or laugh over some joke or pleasantry.

Bill Bryson, Notes from a Small Island (*Yet another American. Charming chap, despite the beard*)

Britain cherishes her eccentrics and wisely holds that the function of government is to build a walled garden in which anarchy can flourish.

Quentin Crisp (*Not at all sure about this feller, though. Went to live in America, as I recall*)

You're allowed to be boring in Britain . . . abroad people expect one to be entertaining.

John Hurt, 1981

The British may not be the greatest nation at winning Winter Olympics, but at least we can carry our bloody flag properly.

Mike Freeman (*Quite. Says it all, really*)

I like a man to be a clean, strong, upstanding Englishman who can look his gnu in the face and put an ounce of lead in it.

P.G. Wodehouse, Mr Mulliner Speaking

Other nations use 'force'; we Britons alone use 'Might'.

Evelyn Waugh, Scoop

Not to be English was for my family so terrible a handicap as almost to place the sufferer in the permanent invalid class.

Osbert Lancaster, All Done from Memory

The English never smash in a face. They merely refrain from asking it to dinner.

Margaret Halsey (1878-1947)

There is in the Englishman a combination of qualities, a modesty, an independence, a responsibility, a repose, combined with an absence of everything calculated to call a blush into the cheek of a young person, which one would seek in vain among the Nations of the Earth.

Charles Dickens, Our Mutual Friend

. . . although it has to be admitted that not *absolutely* everyone is always so enthusiastic about the British – see the penultimate chapter of this book.

Oh, The Joy of
Being in Europe!

Imagine, if you will, sitting at a table in some congenial watering hole, pint of honest English bitter at hand, and just about to tuck into a plate of steaming bangers and mash, of the kind the old Mater – rest her soul – might have dished up. And then, blow me down, some swarthy blighter in an odd-looking suit materializes at your elbow, yells, 'Ces saucissons ne sont pas licites – ils violent la loi européenne!' in a waft of old garlic, and whips your plate away. And just as you're wondering whether to summon the peelers or make the little tick eat his own socks, another feller – this time with an oily black quiff and an even odder suit – grabs your pint, shouts 'Non è birra schietta!' and departs, beer in hand. They then fine you 100 Euros (or 22 pence – whichever is the greater), write out a long ticket in triplicate, and hand it to you. It says, in twelve languages, that you have breached EC Regulation No. Blah-blah-blah, but that you may appeal in the first instance to the Commission in Brussels; if that fails to the Parliament in Strasbourg; and finally to the European Court of Human Rights in The Hague. And you say thank you very much for nothing I don't think, but you'd rather stick to English law if it's all the same to them, and they reply that that's illegal, too. So, they add, is the expression 'English law' – 'un-European', or some other tosh. So you say in that case you'll appeal to the House of Lords, and they snigger unpleasantly, just as you remember that there aren't any proper lords left in Parliament – all there is now, mostly, is a bunch of washed-out former politicians (all of them in pretty suspect suits, too) masquerading as lords and voting each other salaries and quangos and things of that ilk. And that feller who writes musicals. And the advertising johnny (and his family hails from Baghdad). And a few writers and artists and other riff-raff. Creeps and crawlers, the lot of 'em.

Where was I? Oh yes – you think this is a nightmare? Couldn't happen here? Well, all I can say is that you obviously can't have tried to buy any Turkish cigarettes here recently. Consider the list below, and be afraid – be very afraid.

Here are just some of the things those Brussels

bureaucrats are ramming down our throats:

- Pub darts to be banned as dangerous.
- Half the yoghurt sold in Britain to be renamed 'fermented milk'.
- A ban on saucy seaside postcards.
- Farmers must not mow their set-aside fields when wild birds are nesting.
- Village cricket teas to face the axe. (Dangerous, this, I'd have thought. Would leave thousands of Englishwomen with nothing to do on Saturday afternoons. God help us then.)
- In restaurants and cafés, sauces and dressings must be offered in sealed individual sachets rather than bottles and squeezy tubes.
- The hanging of game to tenderize the meat to be banned, or otherwise subjected to impractical controls. Shot game will also have to be free from lead shot [sic].
- Jerrycans[4] to be banned from garage forecourts.
- The sale of homemade bread, jam, etc. to be banned (you may imagine what the Provisional Wing of the Women's Institute –

---

[4] Named after the Germans, whose petrol containers in the last show were a good deal better than our 'flimsies'. We can be fair too, you know.

that's it, the gallant and right-thinking ladies who savaged the Blair creature when he made the mistake of trying to talk down to them – will make of *that*. Rivers of blood mixing with torrents of gooseberry-and-apple in the streets, I shouldn't wonder).

- Professional fishermen must wear hairnets. (To bring them into line with Dutch conscripts, presumably – see footnote, p. 35.)
- Foreign boats permitted to fish for cockles off the Essex coast (their crews no doubt chanting 'Clovisses et moules, en vie, en vie-O' as they heave in their quota-busting catches).
- The Royal Navy's tradition of ratings stirring their Christmas puddings with an oar to be outlawed.
- Street food stalls and vendors and many cafés faced with closure from EC food-hygiene directives.
- Prawn-cocktail- and spring-onion-flavoured crisps banned.
- Paddling pools with a depth greater than 12 inches are EC-classified as swimming pools, and must therefore be attended by a lifeguard (whom the dear little toddlers would maim in pretty short order, if I'm any judge).
- Pork chops cannot be sold with kidneys

attached. (Would have broken my old father's heart – he loved a decent chop with part of a kidney embedded in it. 'Ah, kidneys,' he would bellow, 'good-o! Taste just like their function . . .')

- Doorstep milk deliveries to be banned. (So bang goes your daily 'pinta' – and – who knows? – perhaps your good lady's bit of extramarital hanky-panky, as well.)
- The EC to build a £900 million tower 3,200 feet high to house 20,000 bureaucrats.
- Under EC regulations, wildlife-park tourist signs must carry a picture of an elephant.
- Fishermen must carry condoms in their first-aid kits. (Not sure what this says about fishermen and/or consenting fish. Doesn't bear thinking about.)
- Only authorized aristocrats are permitted to use their titles on the labels of wine bottles.
- EC officials have outlawed the fishy smells in Grimsby. (It is too early to know how the catches brought in by the Grimsby fleet have responded to this edict.)
- Gin bottles must be round in cross-section, not square.

- Political parties to be prohibited from canvassing by post and direct mail.
- Multi-vitamin pills to be banned.
- Advertising on the shells of eggs to be permitted.
- Guy Fawkes Night bonfires to be banned. (Probably just after you'd filled the shops with a hundred dozen eggs printed with the date and venue of your grand Bonfire Night celebration . . .)
- Traditional pizzas outlawed.
- Valentine cards sent to work colleagues infringe EC dignity-at-work recommendations.
- Rural garages forced to close because their petrol pumps are too close to the road.
- British bulldogs, spaniels, corgis and a hundred other favourite British dog breeds to be banned in Europe.
- All milk to be sterilized, thus putting artisan cheesemakers out of business (yet 'Blessèd are the cheesemakers,' according to Monty Python's *Life of Brian*).

And that, I can promise you, is just the tip of the iceberg. The past few years have seen Brussels make attempts upon honest British chocolate bars, sausages, bananas, and a score of other products, either to ban them, modify them, regulate their appearance, contents, taste and so on, or to change our traditional way of describing things. And here's the question you've got to ask yourself. What are they after? And do you trust them?

Then there's the greatest question of all: why do we put up with it, mutely accepting Spanish trawlers hauling out our cod and haddock, and French farmers incinerating our meat lorries? The only thing we ever seem to do in return is ship them a few thousand of our famous football hooligans from time to time, but since the other EC member states have plenty of first-rate hooligans of their own, this is hardly a very effective retaliation. Below are five hundred-odd years' worth of comments about Europe and Europeans, many of them made by foreign johnnies. Makes for pretty sober reading, you'll agree.

There have been many definitions of Hell, but for the English the best definition is that it is the place where the Germans are the police, the Swedish are the comedians, the Italians are the defence force, Frenchmen dig the roads, the Belgians are the pop singers, the Spanish run the

railways, the Turks cook the food, the Irish are
the waiters, the Greeks run the government, and
the common language is Dutch.

David Frost and Antony Jay

In Western Europe there are now only small
countries – those that know it and those that
don't know it yet.

Théo Lefèvre

This going into Europe will not turn out to be the
thrilling mutual exchange supposed. It is more
like nine middle-aged couples with failing
marriages meeting in a darkened bedroom in a
Brussels hotel for a Group Grope.

E.P. Thompson, Sunday Times, *1975 (Except it's
more than nine now)*

In the eyes of the Englishman, the Frenchman is
a dog, the Spaniard a fool, the German a
drunkard, the Italian a bandit, only the
Englishman is the pinnacle of perfection, and
nature's masterpiece.

Riem (1762-1828)

We are with Europe, but not of it. We are linked, but not combined. We are interested and associated, but not absorbed. And should European statesmen address us in the words which were used of old – 'Shall I speak for thee to the King or the Lord of the Host?' – we should reply with the words of the Shunamite woman: 'Nay sir, for we dwell among our own people.'

Winston Churchill, 1950 (*Can't make head or tail of this, to be frank. Still, if the Old Boy said it, then it's good enough for me*)

I once shared a railway compartment between Dunkirk and Brussels with two French-speaking businessmen who were obviously old friends or colleagues. They talked genially the whole journey, but not once in two hours did I see either of them raise a flicker of a smile. You could imagine the same thing with Germans or Swiss or Spaniards or even Italians, but with Britons – never.

Bill Bryson, Notes from a Small Island

Gloria, gloria, Europhoria!
Common faith and common goal!
Meat and milk and wine and butter
Make a smashing casserole!
Let the end of all our striving
Be the peace that love promotes,
With our hands in perfect friendship
Firmly round each other's throats!

Roger Woddis, Spectator, *1984*

European Community institutions have produced
European beets, butter, cheese, wine, veal and
even pigs. But they have not produced Europeans.

Louise Weiss, MEP, Observer, *1980*

The last time Britain went into Europe with any
degree of success was on 6 June 1944.

Daily Express, *1980 (the reference is to the D-Day
landings)*

What Caesar couldn't do, what Charlemagne
couldn't do, what Innocent III and Hitler couldn't

do, it looks like the dough-faced burgher wimps of Brussels might finally be able to pull off – the unification of that portion of the earth's surface known . . . as Europe. What it took a country ten times its size less than a hundred years to accomplish, armed with only machine-guns and a few trillion dollars, it has taken the squabbling, babbling tribes of Europe almost three millennia of wars, migrations, crusades, plague, pillage, partition, diets, dumas, duels, vendettas, incursions, invasions, intrusions, regicides, switching sides and genocide to accomplish.

Tony Hendra, 'EEC! It's the US of E!', National
Lampoon, *1976*

I do not find Northern Europe an ideal zone for human habitation. It is a fine place for industrial productivity, but its climate breeds puritans and the terrible dictates of the Protestant Work Ethic. The Romans were right to pull out when they did.

Kenneth Tynan, The Sound of Two Hands
Clapping, *1975*

Germans are flummoxed by humour, the Swiss have no concept of fun, the Spanish think there is

nothing at all ridiculous about eating dinner at
midnight, and the Italians should never, ever
have been let in on the invention of the motor car.
Bill Bryson, Neither Here Nor There

Frogs . . . are slightly better than Huns or Wops,
but abroad is unutterably bloody and foreigners
are fiends.
Nancy Mitford, The Pursuit of Love

I think he bought his doublet in Italy, his round
hose in France, his bonnet in Germany, and his
behaviour everywhere.
William Shakespeare, The Merchant of Venice

England has saved herself by her exertions, and
will, as I trust, save Europe by her example.
William Pitt, 1805

. . . We'll be subsumed, you see, under
European culture. And what will that be, I ask
myself. A blancmange. More accurately a
cocktail – a bit of this, a bit of that. It will be

Italians in clogs doing the German sausage dance round maypoles. Dame Lynn sings Edith Piaf. Spaniards in kilts, flamenco bars in Glasgow.

'Henry Root' (William Donaldson), Root into Europe

'Subsumed . . . under European culture' – sends a terrible chill down the backbone, doesn't it? Imagine: EC Directive No. XYZ (Amended) on specifications for badger hackles to be worn in Tyrolean hats (which became compulsory for all women between the ages of eighteen and thirty under an earlier Directive); the WI outlawed and driven underground, to be hunted down by Dutch conscripts wearing hairnets (still, not much of a contest there, at least – the night air would be hideous with Netherlandish screams)[5]; Norbert Dentressangle voted most popular boy's name in the annual survey conducted by *The Times*; continued spread of Creeping Continental Caféism – all major city routes in Britain to have

---

[5] Some years ago conscripts in the Royal Netherlands armed forces who chose not to have their hair cut to regulation length were ordered to wear hairnets on parade.

restaurant-table lanes in place of parking bays and bus lanes; Wembley Stadium (if it ever exists again) to be converted for the *corrida* (still, perhaps the banned pub darts could be used against the bulls, thus combining three traditional British virtues: sportsmanship, love of animals, and willingness to compromise); one day's compulsory public bicycling a week for all members of the royal family; traditional British beer and ale to be reclassified as 'Warm Brown Flat Hop-Flavoured Beverage (Warning: contains alcohol)'; first England v. France *boules de pétanque* Test match played at Lord's (France wins by an innings and 100,000 francs) . . .

I rest my case.

Foreign Objects

Many good things have come from 'abroad', over the years. Think of French and Italian wines, Chinese silk, any sort of German machine (like, say, pocket battleships), sherry and port, almost all our footballers, cooking from every corner of the globe (possibly excepting Dutch), paintings and music and books ditto, and so on and so forth.

Nevertheless, there is nowadays a whole raft of foreign objects we can well *do* without, but which people seem increasingly to feel they can't *live* without. As an example, have you been up to Town recently?[6] If you have, you will have noticed that much of the place is stuffed with coffee shops. Go into one, and try ordering a cup of coffee, much less something complicated like a pot of tea for two. You will then be asked a lot of tomfool questions about your choice by an insolent youth with a mid-Atlantic accent. Confused by phrases like 'A tall decaff latte with

_____

[6] You always go up to the capital – even from Inverness.

wings' or 'A large triple-shot cappuccino to fly', you may well find yourself being told to 'Wake up and smell the coffee', meaning that you should 'get your brain in gear'. The whole nonsense is a bewildering and indeed insulting process calculated to render you a) homicidal, and b) coffee-less. All this is the fault of Americans taking over from Italians, and then bringing the whole mongrel caboodle over here. And the sinister thing is that *people seem to like it* . . .

Below are foreign objects to which I especially object. You will have your own *bêtes noires*. Please feel free to add them.

- anything *whatsoever* bearing the words 'Emporio Giorgio Armani'
- back-packers (especially those who use the Tube)
- Bailey's Irish Cream
- bottled water the labels of which bear one or more of the following words: *eau*, *acqua*, *agua* or 'Welsh Spring'
- cappuccino
- ciabatta
- croissants
- French Golden Delicious apples

- Marco-Pierre White
- McDonald's, Burger King and Kentucky Fried Chicken outlets
- Mexican or Spanish beer, especially when offered without a glass, but with a slice of tired fruit rammed into the neck of the bottle
- muesli
- quiche Lorraine
- Ray-Bans
- Rupert Murdoch
- Ruud Gullitt
- Scandinavian furniture (especially of the 'screw-it-together-yourself' variety)
- Spanish trawlers
- tables and chairs set out on pavements outside restaurants and cafés, in a doomed attempt to appear 'Continental'. I call this 'Creeping Continental Caféism', and believe that it should be ruthlessly extirpated (preferably by a half-company of Gurkhas . . .)
- Volkswagen camper vans sporting 'Aus' or 'NZ' stickers
- Welsh male-voice choirs
- whingeing Aussies ('You beat us in a rugger game, so we're not going to let any more of your fans buy tickets for the games': British and Irish Lions tour of Australia, July 2001)

Devolution

The *United* Kingdom? Why devolution is a good idea . . .

. . . for Scotland

It requires a surgical operation to get a joke well into a Scotch understanding.

Sydney Smith

It is never difficult to distinguish between a Scotsman with a grievance and a ray of sunshine.

P.G. Wodehouse

Oats. A grain which in England is generally given to horses, but in Scotland supports the people.

Much may be made of a Scotchman, if he be caught young.

The noblest prospect which a Scotchman ever

sees, is the high road that leads him to England.
Samuel Johnson

Dr Johnson: Sir, it is a very vile country.
Mr S.: Well, Sir, God made it.
Dr Johnson: Certainly he did, but we must
remember that He made it for Scotchmen.
Samuel Johnson, A Journey to the Western
Islands of Scotland

I have been trying all my life to like Scotchmen,
and am obligated to desist from the experiment
in despair.

Charles Lamb

The Scotchman is one who keeps the Sabbath
and every other thing he can lay his hands on.
American saying

Racial characteristics: sour, stingy, depressing
beggars who parade around in schoolgirls' skirts
with nothing on underneath. Their fumbled
attempt at speaking the English language has been
a source of amusement for several centuries, and

their idiot music has been dreaded by those not blessed with deafness for at least as long.

P.J. O'Rourke, National Lampoon, *1976*

There are few more impressive sights in the world than a Scotsman on the make.

J.M. Barrie, What Every Woman Knows

One often yearns
For the land of Burns –
The only snag is
The haggis!

Lils Emslie, Other People's Clerihews

Sex is allowed in Scotland only when Rangers beat Celtic.

Ronnie Barker

The Irish gave the bagpipes to the Scots as a joke, but the Scots haven't seen the joke yet.

Oliver Herford

It is possible that all Scots are illegitimate, Scotsmen being so mean and Scotswomen so generous.

English saying

... for Wales

The earth contains no race of human beings so totally vile and worthless as the Welsh. I have expended in labour, within three years, nearly eight thousand pounds amongst them, yet they treat me as their greatest enemy.

Walter Savage Landor (1775-1864)

Now I perceive the devil understands Welsh.

William Shakespeare, Henry IV *Part 1*

They are treacherous to each other as well as to foreigners, covet freedom, neglect peace, are warlike and skilful in arms, and are eager for revenge.

Walter Map (1140-1209)

Each section of the British Isles has its own way of laughing, except Wales, which doesn't.

Stephen Leacock

A Welshman is a man who prays on his knees on Sunday and preys on his friends the rest of the week.

Traditional saying (*probably English*)

I once heard a Welsh sermon in which the word 'truth' was repeatedly uttered in English. Apparently there is no exact equivalent in Welsh.

Geoffrey Madan

Wales is the land of my fathers. And my fathers can have it.

Dylan Thomas (*who was Welsh. According to Kingsley Amis, Thomas was 'an outstandingly unpleasant man who cheated and stole from his friends and peed on their carpets'*)

We can trace almost all the disasters of English history to the influence of Wales.

The Welsh are the only nation in the world that has produced no graphic or plastic art, no architecture, no drama. They just sing. Sing and blow down instruments of plated silver.

Evelyn Waugh

When asked his opinion of Welsh nationalism, Mr Thomas replied in three words, two of which were 'Welsh nationalism'.

Dylan Thomas (of himself)

There are still parts of Wales where the only concession to gaiety is a striped shroud.

Gwyn Thomas

Names are not always what they seem. The common Welsh name BZJXXLLWCP is pronounced Jackson.

Mark Twain

The ordinary women of Wales are generally
short and squat, ill-favoured and nasty.
David Mallet (1705-65)

... and for Northern Ireland

How about the raffle where the first prize was a
week in Belfast and the second prize was a
fortnight in Belfast?
Brendan Behan (mind you, he was born in
Dublin)

Politics

Quite frankly, our politics are bad enough, without having to contemplate those of other countries. If you don't believe me, take a dekko at what's been said about them over the centuries.

A small acquaintance with history shows that all governments are selfish and the French governments more selfish than most.

Lord Eccles

I do not dislike the French from the vulgar antipathy between neighbouring nations, but for their insolent and unfounded airs of superiority.

Horace Walpole

France was a long despotism tempered by epigrams.

Thomas Carlyle, History of the French Revolution

The French will only be united under the threat of danger. Nobody can simply bring together a country that has 265 kinds of cheese.

Général Charles de Gaulle (who was described by Churchill as looking 'like a female llama who has been surprised in her bath')

France, though armed to the teeth, is pacifist to the core.

Winston Churchill

The simple thing is to consider the French as an erratic and brilliant people . . . who have all the gifts except that of running their country.

James Cameron, News Chronicle, 1954

I have not always in my dealings with General de Gaulle, found quotations from Trafalgar and Waterloo necessarily productive, and he has been very tactful about the Battle of Hastings.

Harold Wilson, 1967

When I want to know what France thinks, I ask myself.

Charles de Gaulle

A French Member of Parliament went to sleep for half an hour during a debate and when he woke up he found he had been Prime Minister twice.

Oswald Lewis

One never hears of a French politician dying – they live for ever ...

... All French politicians love each other, or so they say. They never know when they may want to join each other's governments.

Nancy Mitford, Don't Tell Alfred

One thing I will say for the Germans, they are always perfectly willing to give somebody else's land to somebody else.

Will Rogers (1879-1935)

Ah, so next time we shall not be able to hear them coming.

Pierre Mendès France, former Prime Minister of France, commenting in 1960 on news that German soldiers' boots were now fitted with rubber soles

One German a beer; two Germans an organization; three Germans a war.

Polish saying

I have great admiration for Mussolini, who has welded a nation out of a collection of touts, blackmailers, ice-cream vendors and gangsters.

Michael Bateman

I saw the new Italian navy. Its boats have glass bottoms so they can see the old Italian navy.

Peter Secchia, ex-President George Bush's nominee for US Ambassador to Italy, during Senate confirmation hearings, 1989

Very little counts for less in Italy than the state.
Peter Nichols, Italia, Italia

By 1948 the Italians had begun to pull themselves together, demonstrating once more their astonishing ability to cope with disaster which is so perfectly balanced by their absolute inability to deal with success.
Gore Vidal, Matters of Fact and Fiction

Realizing that they will never be a world power, the Cypriots have decided to be a world nuisance.
George Mikes

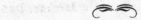

Australia is governed by a hierarchy of hicks.
H.B. Turner, 1970

The Irish, he says, don't care for clean government; they want Irish government.
Stephen Leacock, Arcadian Adventures with the Idle Rich

Gladstone . . . spent his declining years trying to guess the answer to the Irish Question; unfortunately whenever he was getting warm, the Irish secretly changed the Question.

W.C. Sellar and R.J. Yeatman, 1066 and All That

Our ancestors believed in magic, prayers, trickery, browbeating and bullying: I think it would be fair to sum that list up as 'Irish politics'.

Flann O'Brien, The Hair of the Dogma

Politics is the chloroform of the Irish people, or, rather, the hashish.

Oliver St John Gogarty, As I Was Going Down Sackville Street

Food and Drink

For those of the bangers-and-mash, meat-and-two-veg., spotted-dick-with-custard persuasion, here are a few comments about foreign food. Mind you, even I have to admit that we'd be mad to stick only to our national dishes.

The French are sawed-off sissies who eat snails and slugs and cheese that smells like people's feet. Utter cowards who force their own children to drink wine.

P. J. O'Rourke

Everything in France is a pretext for a good dinner.
Jean Anouilh, Cécile

The friendship of the French is like their wine – exquisite, but of short duration.

German saying

Les crudités: genitals
  Andy Kirby, competition, New Statesman, *1985*

The French drink to get loosened up for an event, to celebrate an event, and even to recover from an event.

Geneviève Guérin, French Commission on Alcoholism, 1980

For breakfast, the first morning I was in France, I had a steaming bidet of coffee, followed by porridge and frogs.

Spike Milligan

The French have just invented a Michelin bomb – it destroys only restaurants with less than four stars.

Robin Williams

Paris last year. Wonderful town but the French are awful, the waiters and so on, they're tip mad.
  Tom Stoppard, Neutral Ground

France has found a unique way of controlling its unwanted critter population. They have done this by giving animals like snails, pigeons, and frogs fancy names, thus transforming common backyard pets into expensive delicacies. These are then served to gullible tourists, who will eat anything they can't pronounce; the French could serve *la waddle du gum à la sidewalk* and folks would still gobble it up.

Chris Harris, Don't Go Europe

The French national anthem is 'The Mayonnaise'.
Anon.

When in Paris, I always eat at the Eiffel Tower restaurant because it's the only place where I can avoid seeing the damned thing.

William Morris

How much disgruntled heaviness, lameness, dampness, how much *beer* there is in the German intelligence.

Friedrich Nietzsche, Twilight of the Idols

Three things are in trouble: birds in the hands of
children, young girls in the hands of old men,
and wine in the hands of Germans.

Italian saying

The Prussians have two stomachs and no heart.

German saying

The Germans gorge and swill themselves to
poverty and Hell.

German saying

The Swiss has two bad nights when he can't
sleep – one where he has overloaded his
stomach, and the other where he is lying awake
thinking about how he can overload it again.

German saying

How can we secure food when the Dutchman
spoils what is good?

German saying

A notoriously overweight and idle lot, the Belgians . . . Their customarily bloated expressions are caused by the fact that they carry food around in their cheeks to eat later in the day.

'Henry Root' (William Donaldson), Root into Europe

I don't like Norwegians at all. The sun never sets, the bar never opens, and the whole country smells of kippers.

Evelyn Waugh

Beer is the Danish national drink, and the Danish national weakness is another beer.

Clementine Paddleford (1898-1967)

To speak with your mouth full
And swallow with greed
Are national traits
Of the travelling Swede.

(Alfred) Duff Cooper (1890-1954)

He who would eat in Spain must bring his kitchen along.

German saying

The national dish of America is menus.

Robert Robinson

The bars in Dublin are shut from 2.30 to 3.30. We call it the Holy Hour. The politician who introduced it was shot an hour afterwards.

Brendan Behan

Speech and Language

Aha! Now we come to the pith of the matter –
namely that people from abroad resolutely refuse
to speak, and sometimes even to understand,
plain English. This leaves one in the position of
having to shout even louder in an attempt to
make oneself understood. Exhausting, very.

They [the French] gibber like baboons even when
you try to speak to them in their own wimpy
language.

P. J. O'Rourke

The French do not say what they mean; they do
not read as they write; and they do not sing
according to the notes.

Italian saying

When Frenchmen are talking, never lift the
needle off the gramophone: it only goes back to
the beginning.

Oliver Lyttleton

In Paris they simply stared when I spoke to them in French; I never did succeed in making those idiots understand their own language.

Mark Twain

It is good to be on your guard against an Englishman who speaks French perfectly; he is likely to be a card sharp or an attaché in the diplomatic service.

Somerset Maugham

Imagine the Lord talking French! Apart from a few odd words in Hebrew, I took it completely for granted that God had never spoken anything but the most dignified English.

Clarence Day, Life with Father

No matter how politely or distinctly you ask a Parisian a question he will persist in answering you in French.

Fran Lebowitz, Metropolitan Life

I speak Spanish to God, Italian to women, French to men, and German to my horse.
Charles V, *Holy Roman Emperor (1500-58)*

Life is too short to learn German.
Richard Porson *(1759-1808)*

German is a language which was developed solely to afford the speaker the opportunity to spit at strangers under the guise of polite conversation.
National Lampoon

German is the most extravagantly ugly language – it sounds like someone using a sickbag on a 747.
William Rushton

Whenever the literary German dives into a sentence, that is the last you are going to see of him till he emerges on the other side of his Atlantic with his verb in his mouth.
Mark Twain, A Connecticut Yankee in King Arthur's Court

I can *understand* German as well as the maniac who invented it, but I can *talk* it best through an interpreter.

Mark Twain, A Tramp Abroad

The larger the German body, the smaller the German bathing suit and the louder the German voice issuing German demands and German orders to everybody who doesn't speak German.

P.J. O'Rourke, Holidays in Hell

Metaphysical lederhosen.

D.J. Enright, *of the murky philosophizing and symbolism of German novels*

Dutch is not so much a language as a disease of the throat.

Mark Twain

The American has no language. He has dialect, slang, provincialism, accent and so forth.

Rudyard Kipling

If one could only teach the English how to talk and the Irish how to listen, society would be quite civilized.

Oscar Wilde

There are over thirty words in the Irish language which are equivalent to the Spanish *'mañana'*. But somehow none of them conveys the same sense of urgency.

Patrick Kavanagh

Sex

Personally, I intend to gloss over this section, and on no account should you leave it where your good lady wife might find it. I only include it at Brigadier Arbuthuot's insistence.

French pox and a leather vest last for life.

German saying

It is unthinkable for a Frenchman to arrive at middle age without having syphilis and the Croix de la Légion d'honneur.

André Gide (attrib.)

This sort of thing may be tolerated by the French, but we are British – thank God.

Field Marshal the Viscount Montgomery (on homosexuality)

'American girls do have regrets,' Amy said, 'That is what distinguishes them from French girls.'

Amanda Vail, Love Me Little

She lived in France – that country to which lesbianism is what cricket is to England.

Quentin Crisp

Paris brothels, having been lately driven underground by the ill-considered action of a woman Deputy, had become rather difficult for a foreigner to find.

Nancy Mitford, The Blessing

In America sex is an obsession, in other parts of the world it is a fact.

Marlene Dietrich

The Americans, like the English, probably make love worse than any other race.

Walt Whitman

Australians are still too conservative for
anatomically correct dolls.
Spokesman for the Australian toy trade, 1969

In Ireland a girl has the choice between perpetual
virginity and perpetual pregnancy.
George Moore

Traditional Sayings

The interesting thing about these is that only one of them originated in this country. Most are historical, and refer to times when one or other country was able to dominate its neighbours. Still, they do show that envy or resentment of other countries is far from being an Anglo-Saxon trait.

He lies like a French bulletin.

Dutch saying

It took no more effort than casting a Frenchman into Hell.

Dutch saying

Attila, the scourge of God; the French his brothers.

Italian saying

[About the French] They do everything and know nothing.

Italian saying

A fighting Frenchman runs away from even a she-goat.

Russian saying

Marry a German and you'll see that the women have hairy tongues.

Ruthenian saying

When a snake warms himself on ice, a German will begin to wish a Czech well.

Czech saying

Rather die with Denmark than rot with Prussia.

Danish saying

Wherever Germans are, it is unhealthy for Italians.

Italian saying

Better Turkish hatred than German love.

Croatian saying

With the Germans friendship make, but as neighbours do not take.

German saying

The German lies as soon as he becomes polite.

German saying

The German is as sly as the plague.

Polish saying

The German may be as big as a poplar tree, but he is as stupid as a bean.

Polish saying

A dead German, a dead dog; the difference is but slight.

Polish saying

German goods are fragile and German words deceptive.

Finnish saying

God guard us against the health of the Germans and the malady of the French.

French saying

Italy is Paradise for horses and Hell for women.

German saying

Italian devotion and German fasting have no meaning.

Danish saying

Italian soup.

Czech term for poison

To cook an egg, to make a bed for a dog, and to teach an Italian to do anything are three hard things.

German saying

Cross yourself once before an Andalusian and thrice on spotting an Italian.

Spanish saying

Half an Italian is one too many in a house.

Traditional French and German insult

Italy is a paradise inhabited by devils.

Traditional German saying

An ass in Germany is a professor in Rome.

Traditional German saying

If there is a Hell, Rome is built on top of it.

German saying

No more money, no more Swiss.

French saying

You may as well bang your head into a wall as talk to a Swiss.

French saying

In a Spanish inn, you will find only what you have brought there yourself.

French saying

He speaks French like a Spanish cow.

French saying

The only good thing that comes from the east is the sun.

> **Portuguese saying** (NB: Spain is to the east of Portugal)

The Spaniard is a bad servant, but a worse master.

> **English saying**

A Spaniard may be trusted – but no further than your nose.

> **German saying**

Spanish are like lice – once they are there it is difficult to get rid of them.

> **German saying**

A Spaniard and a braggart are the same thing.

> **German saying**

Holland is a country where the earth is better than the air, where profit is sought more than humour; where there is more sense than *esprit*; where there is more goodwill than good humour; where there is more prosperity than humour; and where a visit is preferable to living.

German saying

A dark German, a blond Italian and a red Spaniard seldom mean well, like a Dutchman of any colour.

German saying

Finland is the Devil's country.

Russian saying

A crab is no fish, and a Greek is no man.

Russian saying

The Greeks tell the truth, but only once a year.

Russian saying

After shaking hands with a Greek, count your
fingers.

Albanian saying

A Greek can only be cheated by the Devil.

Greek saying

All Cretans are liars.

Greek saying

A Jew thinks first of wife and child; a Pole thinks
first of horse and dog.

Yiddish saying

Love without jealousy is like a Pole without lice.

French saying

The Alps divide us from the Italians,
From the French the river separates us,
The sea is between us and the English,
But only hate keeps us and the Poles apart.

German rhyme

Where the women are stronger than the men.
> **Russian saying** (*of Russia*)

How can you tell a Russian? Go to sleep and he will rob you.

> **Ukrainian saying**

If a Russian is in the hills count your olives.

> **Greek saying**

The Russian knows the way, yet he asks for directions.

> **Ukrainian saying**

If a Russian tells you it's dry, put your collar up.

> **Ukrainian saying**

Better the Devil in your house than a Russian.

> **Ukrainian saying**

A Little Englander's Miscellany

Or 'Home Thoughts About Abroad', as that wild ass Robert Browning might have put it . . . Mind you, there's the odd dig at us, too.

In America, only the successful writer is important, in France all writers are important, in England no writer is important, and in Australia you have to explain what a writer is.

Geoffrey Cottrell

Should the French dare invade us, thus armed with our poles,
We'll bang their bare ribs, make their lantern jaws ring:
For your beef-eating, beer-drinking Britons are souls
Who will shed their last blood for their country and King.

Drinking song, c. 1757

The Americans have need of the telephone, but we do not. We have plenty of messenger boys.
Sir William Preece, chief engineer of the Post Office, 1876

MEPs have been told to shower more often because problems have emerged with the showers installed in the new Parliament building in Strasbourg. They leak if underused.

The softer the currency in a foreign country, the harder the toilet paper.
John Fountain

A gesticulation is any movement made by a foreigner.
J. B. Morton

What do I think of Western civilization? I think it would be a very good idea.
Mahatma Gandhi

When the missionaries came to Africa they had
the Bible and we had the land. They said 'Let us
pray.' We closed our eyes. When we opened
them we had the Bible and they had the land.

Archbishop Desmond Tutu

It is suicide to be abroad.

Samuel Beckett _(Irish born, but settled in Paris._
Says it all, really . . .)

It is easy to be rude on the Continent. You just
shout and call people names of a zoological
character.

George Mikes, How To Be An Alien

England and America are two countries divided
by a common language.

George Bernard Shaw

When an American heiress wants to buy a man,
she at once crosses the Atlantic. The only really

materialistic people I have ever met are the Europeans.

Mary McCarthy

I don't hold with abroad and think that foreigners speak English when our backs are turned.

Quentin Crisp

In an undeveloped country don't drink the water, in a developed country don't breathe the air.

Jonathan Raban, Reader's Digest

The Little Englander's Gazetteer

I have compiled this section in order to provide the true xenophobe with handy quotations for almost any situation when abroad, and especially in Europe. A word of warning, however: be sure to keep a large table between yourself and whoever you may be addressing . . .

France

The ignorance of French society gives one a rough sense of the infinite.

Joseph E. Renan (1823-92)

They are short, blue-vested people who carry their own onions when cycling abroad, and have a yard which is 3.37 inches longer than other people's.

Alan Coren

France is a country where the money falls apart in your hands and you can't tear the toilet paper
Billy Wilder

Frenchmen resemble apes, who, climbing up a tree from branch to branch, never cease going till they come to the highest branch, and there show their bare behinds.

Michel Eyquem de Montaigne

They aren't much good at fighting wars any more. Despite their reputation for fashion, their women have spindly legs. Their music is sappy. But they do know how to whip up a plate of grub.

Mike Royko

Our nation is divided into two species: the one of idle monkeys who mock at everything; and the other of tigers who tear.

Voltaire (1694-1778)

The Almighty in His infinite wisdom did not see fit
to create Frenchmen in the image of Englishmen.
Winston Churchill

A middle-aged, heterosexual, college-educated
male wearing a Mickey Mouse T-shirt and a
string-bikini bottom and carrying a purse – what
else could it be but a vacationing Frenchman? No
tropical shore is too stupid for the French. They
turn up on the coasts of Angola, Eritrea,
Bangladesh and Sri Lanka. For one day they glory
in *l'atmosphère très primitive*, then spend two weeks
in an ear-splitting snit because the natives won't
make a *steak frite* out of the family water buffalo . . .

. . . French women, whether pretty or not, all
walk around with their noses in the air (and
pretty big noses they usually are). I guess this is
what's meant by their 'sense of style'. Where did
this sense of style thing get started? The French
are a smallish, monkey-looking bunch and not
dressed any better, on average, than the citizens
of Baltimore.

P.J. O'Rourke, Holidays in Hell

Britain has football hooligans, Germany has neo-Nazis, and France has farmers.

The Times, *1992*

Pas de deux: father of twins.
Coup de grâce: lawnmower

Fin de siècle: tail light of a bicycle.

Russell Lucas, *competition*, New Statesman,
1985

Esprit de corps: embalming fluid.

R. S. Macleod, *competition*, New Statesman,
1985

Hors de combat: camp follower
Sangfroid: bloody cold

Oh, how I love Humanity,
With love so pure and pringlish,

84

And how I hate the horrid French,
Who never will be English!
         G.K. Chesterton, *'The World State'*

France is the largest country in Europe, a great
boon for drunks, who need room to fall . . .
         Alan Coren, The Sanity Inspector

But there's always something fishy about
the French!
Whether Prince or Politician
We've a sinister suspicion
That behind their *savoir-faire*
They share
A common contempt
For every mother's son of us.
         Noël Coward, song from Conversation Piece,
                                    1934

Probably the worst xenophobes on earth are the
French, a nation protected by a cloud of garlic
breath which still built the Maginot Line to keep
foreigners out. Chauvinism is a French word

which cannot be translated, so Froggie is the emotion it describes.

The National Lampoon Encyclopaedia of Humor, *1973*

The French invented the only known cure for dandruff. It is called the guillotine.

P. G. Wodehouse

To be a Frenchman abroad is to be miserable.

Ambrose Bierce

Going to the loo in a yacht in a French harbour is not so much goodbye as *au revoir*.

Noël Coward

The French are tremendous snobs, despite that rather showy and ostentatious Revolution.

Arthur Marshall, I'll Let You Know

In France you are always in a witness box . . . You must sharpen your wits if you want a favourable verdict.

Nancy Mitford, The Blessing

My attitude to France was, I suppose, inherited
from my father, who always felt perfectly at
home there because he never attempted to talk or
make friends with the natives.

Robert Morley, A Musing Morley

To watch a Frenchman pay for something is to
watch him die a slow death.

Robert Morley, Observer

'HOP OFF YOU FROGS'

*Badge produced by the Sun during the 'Lamb
War' in 1984*

Germany

The river Rhine, it is well known,
Doth wash your city of Cologne;
But tell me, Nymphs, what power divine
Shall henceforth wash the river Rhine?

Samuel Taylor Coleridge, 'Cologne'

One of the greatest crimes of the Germans is that they work too hard. The English – quite rightly – can never forgive them for this . . .

. . . If you want to be a good German, you must have a grudge . . .

. . . The British dislike the Germans because they have their hair cropped in a funny way; because they eat sandwiches with a knife and fork; because they are formal, stiff and click their heels; and because they work too hard and take themselves deadly seriously.

George Mikes, Über Alles – Germany Explored

The great virtues of the German people have created more evils than idleness ever did vices.

Paul Valéry (1871-1945)

The German – as opposed to the human – mind.

William James (1842-1910)

The German mind has a talent for making no mistakes but the very greatest.

Clifton Fadiman

'Don't Let's Be Beastly to the Germans.'
Noël Coward, song title

How appallingly thorough these Germans always managed to be, how emphatic! In sex no less than in war – in scholarship, in science. Diving deeper than anyone else, and coming up muddier.
Aldous Huxley

They are a fine people but quick to catch the disease of anti-humanity. I think it's because of their poor elimination. Germany is a headquarters for constipation.
George Grosz

The German people are an orderly, vain, deeply sentimental and rather insensitive people. They seem to feel at their best when they are singing in chorus, saluting or obeying orders.
H.G. Wells, Travels of a Republican Radical in Search of Hot Water

I was taught to regard Germany as a very serious place because I was a little Irish Protestant and knew that Martin Luther was a German. I therefore concluded that all Germans went to Heaven, an opinion which I no longer hold with any conviction.

George Bernard Shaw, What I Owe to German Culture

If one had to be foreign it was far better to be German, preferably a Prussian . . . Indeed had the Germans only possessed a sense of humour they might almost have qualified as honorary Englishmen.

Osbert Lancaster, All Done from Memory

A German plants seven rose trees on the north side and seven on the south, and if they do not grow up all the same size and shape it worries him so that he cannot sleep . . .

. . . In Germany you must not wear fancy dress in the streets. A Highlander of my acquaintance spent the first few days of his residence in Dresden arguing this question with the government.

Jerome K. Jerome, Three Men on the Bummel *(this rule, however, clearly doesn't apply to Germans, who like nothing better than to appear in public in an embroidered shirt, lederhosen, and a little hat with a badger hackle in it . . .)*

A German's relationship with leather is absolutely of the essence. It has been calculated that ninety-five per cent of German men wear leather body stockings under their working clothes. Your German's preferred way of letting off steam after personally turning out thirty-five Mercedes saloon cars in a day is as follows: after work he'll shower at home and change his body stocking. Alternatively, he'll lie on a hot slab in a bathhouse and have his backside twigged . . . Then he's ready to put on shorts and do the sausage dance in company. Several buckets of lager later, he'll spew up, exit with his pals and form a priapic pyramid in the street.

'Henry Root' (William Donaldson), Root into Europe

'THE SUN INVADES GERMANY'
*Headline in the **Sun**, 1987*

Italy

The median Italian . . . is a cowardly baritone
who consumes 78.3 kilometres of carbohydrates
a month and drives about in a car slightly
smaller than he is, looking for a divorce.
>   ***Alan Coren***, The Sanity Inspector

Italy is a geographical expression.
>   ***Prince Metternich***

No Italian priest
Shall tithe or toll in our dominions.
>   ***William Shakespeare***, King John

An English army led by an Irish general: that
might be a match for a French army led by an
Italian general.
>   ***George Bernard Shaw***, The Man of Destiny

It is peculiar that all the sights in Rome are called
after London cinemas.
>   ***Nancy Mitford***

Q: How is the Italian version of Christmas different?
A: One Mary, one Jesus, and thirty-two Wiseguys.

Q: How does an Italian get into an honest business?
A: Usually through the skylight.

Q: What does FIAT stand for?
A: Frenzied Italian At Traffic lights.

Q: What is an innuendo?
A: An Italian suppository.

Q: Why are most Italian-American men named Tony?
A: When they got on the boat to New York they stamped 'To NY' on their foreheads.

A lady gets on a bus in New York and sits down in front of two Italian men. She overhears the following:

'Emma come first, then I come. Two assa comma together. I come again. Two assa comma together again. I pee twice. I come again.'

The woman turns around and says indignantly:

93

'In our country we don't talk about our sex lives in public!'

'Ah, lady,' says the man. 'I'ma just learnin' to spell "Mississippi".'

Switzerland

In Italy for thirty years under the Borgias they had warfare, terror, murder, bloodshed – they produced Michelangelo, Leonardo da Vinci and the Renaissance. In Switzerland they had brotherly love, five centuries of democracy and peace and what did they produce . . . ? The cuckoo clock.

Orson Welles, The Third Man

Since both its [Switzerland's] national products, snow and chocolate, melt, the cuckoo clock was invented solely in order to give tourists something solid to remember it by.

Alan Coren

A country to be in for two hours, or two and a half if the weather is fine, and no more. Ennui comes in the third hour, and suicide attacks you before the night.

Lord Brougham *(1778-1868)*

I don't like Switzerland – it has produced
nothing but theologians and waiters.

Oscar Wilde

Switzerland has produced the numbered bank
account, Ovaltine and Valium.

Peter Freedman

Switzerland is a curst, selfish, swinish country of
brutes, placed in the most romantic region of the
world.

Lord Byron

The train passed fruit farms and clean villages
and Swiss cycling in kerchiefs, calendar scenes
that you admire for a moment before feeling an
urge to move on to a new month.

Paul Theroux, The Great Railway Bazaar

Switzerland is simply a large, humpy, solid rock, with a thin skin of grass stretched over it.

Mark Twain, A Tramp Abroad

Holland

The Dutch fall into two quite distinct physical types – the small, corpulent, red-faced Edams and the thinner, paler, larger Goudas . . .

. . . Apart from cheese and tulips, the main product of Holland is advocaat, a drink made from lawyers.

Alan Coren

Compared with Greece and Italy, Holland is but a platter-faced, cold-gin-and-water country, after all, and a heavy, barge-built, web-footed race are its inhabitants.

Sir Francis Bond Head (1793-1875)

Amsterdam poses a triple threat; drugs, sex and pollution. The indigenous population is as high as kites on substances and the place is sinking at the rate of six feet per annum. Largely the fault of our good selves, I'm glad to say. Thanks to toxic emissions from the UK, the sea level is rising steadily, with the satisfactory result that Amsterdam will have disappeared entirely by the year 2050. And not before time in my opinion.

'Henry Root' (William Donaldson), Root into Europe

Holland . . . lies so low they're only saved by being dammed.

Thomas Hood (1799-1845)

Belgium

Ethnically disadvantaged (adj.) – anyone born in Belgium

Mike Lepine and Mark Leigh, The Official Politically Incorrect Handbook

Q: Who won Belgium's national beauty contest?
A: Nobody.

Scandinavia

(Well, and Finland too . . .)

[On Denmark] I see nothing here but ruins.
Mary Wollstonecraft (1759-97)

Something is rotten in the state of Denmark.
William Shakespeare, Hamlet

[On Sweden] It's where they commit suicide and
the king rides a bicycle.

Alan Bennett, Enjoy

Louise: You were champion of all Finland?
Sven: Well. Nearly all Finland. There were some
parts of Finland that didn't compete. Let us say,
most of Finland.

Alan Ayckbourn, Joking Apart

Q: Why does the Swede hate washing windows?
A: It takes so long to dig down the ladder . . .

After the end of the Russo-Finnish War, a young female reporter from a British newspaper was sent to Finland to write an article about the soldiers' homecoming. She had interviewed half a dozen servicemen, when she met Pekka on the street.

'Excuse me,' she said 'but were you in the war?'

'Yah, I was in the infantry.'

'Would you mind answering a few questions for a newspaper article?'

'Nej, I wouldn't mind at all.'

'Thank you. So – when you came home, after the war was over, what was the first thing you did?'

'I fucked my wief,' Pekka said bluntly. The journalist went crimson, and tried desperately to change the subject.

'After that. I mean, what did you do after that?' she said hurriedly.

'I fucked her again,' he answered. The embarrassed journalist turned, if possible, even redder, and became even more desperate to change the subject.

'Other than that! Um – what did you do when you had finished with all that?!'

'Then I unstrapped my skis and my heavy backpack.'

Greece

The Greeks – dirty and impoverished descendants of a bunch of la-de-da fruit salads who invented democracy and then forgot how to use it while walking around dressed up like girls.

P.J. O'Rourke

Few things can be less tempting or less dangerous than a Greek woman of the age of thirty.

John Carne (1906-96)

Q: What do you call a Greek girl who keeps running away from home?
A: A virgin.

Poland

Poland is now a totally independent nation, and it has managed to greatly improve its lifestyle thanks to the introduction of modern Western conveniences such as food.

Dave Barry

There are few virtues which the Poles do not possess and there are few errors they have ever avoided.

Winston Churchill

Q: Why did the Pole buy his wife a wig?
A: He heard that she was getting balled at the office.

Q: Did you hear about the Polish man who can't spell?
A: Every payday he spends all night at a warehouse.

Russia

In Russia, a man is called reactionary if he objects to having his property stolen and his wife and children murdered.

Winston Churchill

Russia scares me – the people on the buses are so serious they look like they're going to the electric chair.

Muhammad Ali, 1978

Moscow is the only city where, if Marilyn Monroe walked down the street with nothing on but a pair of shoes, people would stare at her feet first.

John Gunther, 1962

One Russian is an anarchist, two Russians are a chess game, three Russians are a revolution, and four Russians are the Budapest String Quartet.

Jascha Heifetz (who was born in Lithuania – then a subject state of the Russian Empire – in 1901, fled St Petersburg and the Russian Revolution in 1917, and settled in America. So he ought to have known . . .)

Students of Soviet affairs know how difficult it is to foretell the Soviet past.

George Paloczi-Horvath

The Russian is a delightful person till he tucks in his shirt. As an oriental he is charming. It is only when he insists on being treated as the most easterly of western peoples instead of the most westerly of easterns that he becomes a racial anomaly extremely difficult to handle.

Rudyard Kipling

From being a patriotic myth, the Russian people have become an awful reality.

Leon Trotsky (whose name, in reality, was Lev Davidovich Bronstein)

Q: Why, in America, is two-day-old sour cream considered spoiled, while in Russia even two-week-old sour cream is still considered good?
A: What is two weeks to Russia, with its magnificent history of so many centuries?

Q: What is the hottest item in Russian department stores?
A: Underwear labelled: January, February, March, April . . .

Q: What's two miles long and vegetarian?
A: A meat queue in Moscow!

A chambermaid in a Moscow hotel during Soviet times came upon a tourist watering flowers in his hotel room.

'Please don't water the flowers,' she implored. 'The microphone will rust.'

A friend visited the home of a Russian cosmonaut and found only the children there.

'Where are your parents?' the guest inquired. 'Will they be home soon?'

'Father is on a space flight,' they replied. 'He'll be home soon. But Mother went to the store to buy butter. We don't expect her for some time.'

At the height of the Cold War, two Russian military strategists were discussing the tactics to be employed in the event of war with the Western powers.

'If there is war,' said one, 'we will have agents carry nuclear bombs concealed in suitcases to all the capitals and major cities of the Western world: New York, Washington, London, Paris, Bonn . . . '

'That's an excellent idea, Comrade General,' replied his companion. 'We certainly have enough bombs for that. But where are we going to get all those suitcases?'

A Party delegation was visiting a school to see how the indoctrination of children was progressing.

'Tell me, Ivan,' asked a commissar, 'Who is your father?'

'My father is the all-powerful Soviet Union.'

'Very good. Now, my little comrade,' the commissar said, 'Who is your mother?'

'My mother is the ever-present Communist Party,' replied the pupil.

'Excellent, Ivan, excellent!' praised the commissar. 'And what do you want to be when you grow up?'

'An orphan.'

A Muscovite was shopping for a new car. After weeks of looking, he found the car of his dreams. During final negotiations, he asked when he could pick it up. The dealer told him that he could come and get it promptly on 4 September, at 9 a.m . . . in the year 2011. This upset the man a lot, which he mentioned to the dealer. The dealer told him that ten years wasn't that long to wait for a car in Moscow. The customer replied that the year 2011 wasn't the problem; it was 4 September at 9 a.m.

'That,' he explained, 'is when the plumber is scheduled to arrive.'

Trying to borrow money from the World Bank, the Soviet Finance Minister was asked what he could put up for collateral.

'Well,' he said, 'we have countless deposits of oil and minerals such as gold and silver.'

'Those are all underground,' the bank's representative replied. 'What do you have above ground?'

Inflating his chest, the minister said, 'We have superb Russian leaders.'

Profoundly unimpressed, the banker answered, 'You can have your loan, Minister, when the two assets change places.'

On a visit to the West, a Soviet citizen was besieged with many questions from people wanting to know more about communism.

'You mean to tell me,' asked a curious host, 'that by being a communist you share everything?'

'Yes,' came the reply.

'You mean if you had two houses, you would give me one?'

'Of course.'

'And if you had two cars, you would give me one?'

'Certainly.'

'And if you had two stoves, or TVs, or refrigerators, you would give me one of each?'

'Naturally'

'And if you had two shirts, would you give me one?'

'No!' replied the communist emphatically.

'Why not?'

'Because I have two shirts!'

A Russian couple was walking down the street in Moscow one night, when the man felt a drop of moisture hit his nose.

'I think it's raining,' he said to his wife.

'No, that felt more like snow to me,' she replied.

'No, I'm sure it was just rain,' he said.

Well, as these things go, they were about to have a major argument about whether it was raining or snowing. Just then they saw a minor Communist Party official walking toward them.

'Let's not fight about it,' the man said, 'Let's ask Comrade Rudolf whether it is officially raining or snowing.'

As the official approached, the man asked, 'Tell us, Comrade Rudolf, is it officially raining, or snowing?'

'It's raining, of course,' he replied curtly, and walked on. Yet still the woman insisted, 'I know that it felt like snow!'

The man quietly replied, 'Rudolf the Red knows rain, dear!'

A train, travelling across the Soviet Union, suddenly stops because there are no tracks in front. What would each of the former Soviet leaders do?

Lenin would make everyone get out of the train to work for the next 200 hours until they had figured something out.

Stalin would order everyone in the first car to be shot, and everyone else to be shot unless they got the train moving by the next morning.

Khrushchev would order that the tracks behind be taken up and laid down in front of the train.

Brezhnev would have all the window blinds closed and order everyone to rock the cars, so as to give an impression of movement.

Andropov would order the KGB to investigate the entire Soviet railway system, and have himself flown out by military helicopter.

Gorbachev would do nothing other than get everyone to go outside and yell loudly, 'We ain't got the rails and not even any food in the restaurant car.'

Yeltsin would order the army to attack the Russian Parliament and hope that everyone would forget about the train incident.

America

Americans are like a rich father who wishes he knew how to give his son the hardships that made him rich.

Robert Frost

Their demeanour is invariably morose, sullen, clownish, and repulsive. I should think there is not, on the face of the earth, a people so entirely destitute of humour, vivacity or the capacity for enjoyment.

Charles Dickens

I never saw an American man walk or stand well; they are nearly all hollow-chested and round-shouldered.

Frances Trollope (1780-1863)

Of course, America had often been discovered before Columbus, but it had always been hushed up.

Oscar Wilde

It was wonderful to find America, but it would have been more wonderful to miss it.

Mark Twain

America is a mistake, a giant mistake!

Sigmund Freud

It is by the goodness of God that in our country we have those three unspeakably precious things: freedom of speech, freedom of conscience and the prudence never to practise either of them.

Mark Twain

America . . . where laws and customs alike are based on the dreams of spinsters.

Bertrand Russell

America is a large, friendly dog in a very small room. Every time it wags its tail it knocks over a chair.

Arnold Toynbee

America is the only nation in history which miraculously has gone from barbarism to degeneration without the usual interval of civilization.

Georges Clemenceau

There's no underestimating the intelligence of the American public.
H. L. Mencken (who was, of course, American)

No one can be as calculatedly rude as the British, which amazes Americans, who do not understand studied insult and can only offer abuse as a substitute.

Paul Gallico

The American male doesn't mature until he has exhausted all other possibilities.

Wilfrid Sheed, Office Politics

Americans always try to do the right thing ... after they have tried everything else

Winston Churchill (*who was himself half American*)

I am willing to love all mankind, except an American

Samuel Johnson

As for marriage, it is one of America's most popular institutions. The American man marries early and the American woman marries often; and they get on extremely well together.

Oscar Wilde

Americans hardly ever retire from business; they are either carried out feet first or they jump from a window.

A. L. Goodheart

My ancestors were Puritans from England. They arrived in the United States in 1648 in the hope of finding greater restrictions than were permissible under English law at that time.

Garrison Keillor

America has become so tense and nervous, it's been years since I've seen anyone asleep in church.

Norman Vincent Peale

American newspapers are too big, and their lavatory paper too small.

Ernest Bevin (there is an obvious answer to the Labour politician's problem, but it doesn't seem to have struck him . . .)

In the Soviet Union a writer who is critical is taken to a lunatic asylum. In the United States, he is taken to a talk show.

Carlos Fuentes

Americans are a race of convicts and ought to be thankful for anything we allow them short of hanging.

Samuel Johnson

America is the land of permanent waves and impermanent wives.

Brendan Behan

Canada

Canadians are Americans with no Disneyland.
Margaret Mahy, The Changeover

I see Canada as a country torn between a very northern, rather extraordinary, mystical spirit which it fears and its desire to present itself to the world as a Scotch banker.

> **Robertson Davies**, The Enthusiasms of
> Robertson Davies

Canada could have enjoyed English government, French culture and American know-how. Instead it ended up with English know-how, French government and American culture.

> **John Robert Colombo**

I was in a library in Toronto in 1915, studying a Latin poet, and all of a sudden I thought, war can't be this bad. So I walked out and enlisted.

> **Lester B. Pearson**

Canada is a country so square that even the female impersonators are women.

> **Richard Brenner**

For some reason, a glaze passes over people's faces when you say Canada.

> **Sondra Gotleib**

I don't even know what block it's on.

Al Capone, *of Canada, when it was suggested that he should flee there to escape the US tax investigators who were closing in on him*

This gloomy region, where the year is divided into one day and one night, lies entirely outside the stream of history.

W.W. Reade, 1872

So this is Winnipeg. I can tell it's not Paris.

Bob Edwards

The Niagara Falls is simply a vast, unnecessary amount of water going the wrong way and then falling over unnecessary rocks.

Oscar Wilde (Decades later, Winston Churchill was clearly irritated at being asked if the Niagara Falls looked the same as when he had first seen them. 'Well, the principle seems the same. The water still keeps falling over,' he growled.)

In any world menu, Canada must be considered the vichyssoise of nations. It's cold, half-French, and difficult to stir.

Stuart Keate

Australia

To live in Australia permanently is rather like going to a party and dancing all night with your mother.

Barry Humphries *(an Australian, you may care to note . . .)*

Australia is a country whose industrial and commercial development has been unspeakably retarded by an unfortunate dispute among geographers as to whether it is a continent or an island.

Ambrose Bierce

I was the toast of two continents – Greenland and Australia.

Dorothy Parker

The high standards of Australians are due to the fact that their ancestors were all hand-picked by the best English judges.

Douglas Copeland

Really nice . . . it made the spirits sink . . .

. . . And it didn't seem to be real. It seemed to be sprinkled on the surface of a darkness into which it never penetrated.

D.H. Lawrence, Kangaroo *(of Australia. He seems to have had an impassioned hatred for anything he considered to be 'nice'.)*

So you're going to Australia! . . . What are you going to sing? All I can say is – sing 'em muck! It's all they can understand!

Dame Nellie Melba, *Australian soprano, speaking to the English contralto Clara Butt*

Australia is a huge rest home, where no unwelcome news is ever wafted on to the pages of the worst newspapers in the world.

Germaine Greer

Once you've been on a plane full of drunken Australians doing wallaby imitations up and down the aisles, you'll never make fun of Americans again.

P.J. O'Rourke

Well, it's [the film's] about the end of the world, and God knows, this place is the absolute end.

Ava Gardner, *talking to Australian pressmen about the film* On the Beach, *in which she starred with Gregory Peck*

Xenophobia: a love of Australia.

Barry Humphries, Bazza Pulls It Off

Australian-based: a person who has been

successfully bribed with grants and awards to
resist the lure of expatriation.

Barry Humphries, A Nice Night's
Entertainment

It is Wembley in South-East Asia; a tropical
Manchester.

Barry Humphries, Punch Down Under

Racial characteristics: violently loud alcoholic
roughnecks whose idea of fun is to throw up on
your car. The national sport is breaking furniture
and the average daily consumption of beer in
Sydney is ten and three-quarters Imperial gallons
for children under the age of nine.

P.J. O'Rourke, National Lampoon

Australia!
   Land of ravaged desert, shark-infested ocean
and thirst-lashed outback.
   Australia!
   Land of strange, exotic creatures, freaks of
evolution, ghastly victims of Mother Nature's
vicious whimsy – kangaroo and platypus,

potoroo and bandicoot, Richie Benaud and . . .
Peter Tinniswood, The Brigadier Down Under

The Duchess of Berwick: Do you know, Mr
Hopper, dear Agatha and I are so much
interested in Australia. It must be so pretty with
all the dear little kangaroos flying about.
Oscar Wilde, Lady Windermere's Fan

A broad school of Australian writing has based
itself on the assumption that Australia not only has
a history worth bothering about, but that all history
worth bothering about happened in Australia.
Clive James, The Dreaming Swimmer

First World War British general (addressing
Australian troops newly arrived in the front
line): 'Did you come here to die?'
Digger: No, mate, we came yester-die.

Q. What's the great Australian dream?
A. Every Pommie swimming out of Sydney

Harbour with a New Zealander under each arm.

New Zealand

Terrible Tragedy in the South Seas. Three million people trapped alive!

Tom Scott, Listener

New Zealand is a country of thirty thousand million sheep – three million of whom think they are human.

Barry Humphries

A bloke went into the fish shop and asked for some 'fush n' chups'.

'Ar! You're a Kiwi, eh?' said the proprietor. The New Zealander was sick and tired of this, so he spent the next three months at an elocution class.

He finally returned to the shop and asked, in perfect English for some 'fish and chips'.

'Ar! You're a Kiwi, eh?'

'How the hell did you know that?'

'Because this has been a hardware store for the last two weeks.'

The New Zealand couple finally worked out a solution to the eternal love triangle.

They ate the sheep.

The Kiwi farmer's wife gave him a plate of grass for his dinner.

'What the hell's this?' he exploded.

'If its good enough for your girlfriend, then it's good enough for you!' she replied.

The Far East

I don't greatly admire Japanese women; they have no figures to speak of, and look as if a bee had stung them in the eye.

Crosbie Garstin, The Dragon and the Lotus

Our trouble is that we drink too much tea. I see in this the slow revenge of the Orient, which has diverted the Yellow River down our throats.

J.B. Priestley (*Actually, in the nineteenth century we – the British, that is – diverted the tea from China*

to India, and the opium from India to China. When
the Chinese objected to this state-sanctioned drug
running and refused to open their ports to the opium
trade, we dusted them up in two wars, known as the
Opium Wars . . .)

I found the Pearl of the Orient slightly less
exciting than a rainy Sunday evening in
Rochester.
> **S.J. Perelman** *(that's Rochester, New Jersey, of*
> *course)*

The Japanese have almost as big a reputation for
cruelty as do young children.
> **Dennis Bloodworth** *(1718-80)*

There are two kinds of Chinese – those who give
bribes, and those who take them.
> **Russian saying**

In January, the Americans announce a new
invention. In February, the Russians announce
they made the same discovery twenty years ago.

In March, the Japanese start exporting it to the US.

Lloyd Cory

The Koreans have been called 'The Irish of the East', but this is an insult to the Irish.

James Kirkup, Streets of Asia

Q. How do you know when your house has been robbed by an oriental gang member?
A. The dog is missing and your homework has been done.

Outside an hotel near Oxford Street, a Japanese tourist hails a cab and tells the driver to take him to the airport. On their way, a car zooms by and the Japanese goes, 'Aaah! Toyota, made in Japan, very faaast!' And then another car zooms by and the Japanese goes, 'Aaah! Nissan, made in Japan, very faaast!' And then yet another car zooms by and the Japanese goes, 'Aaah! Mitsubishi, made in Japan, very faaast!' By this time, the cabby is getting very tired of this exhibition of nationalistic pride. Upon arriving at the airport, he tells his passenger, 'One hundred pounds, please . . . '

The Japanese is shocked. 'One hundred pounds?! It's not that far from the hotel!' he complains.

'Aaah! Taxi meter, made in Japan, very faaast!'

Three samurai met to decide which among them was the greatest swordsman.

The judge approached the first samurai and opened a small box. Out flew a fly. The samurai's sword flashed through the air and the fly fell to the ground, neatly sliced in half.

'Very impressive,' said the judge. Now he turned to the second samurai and again opened a small box. The samurai's sword flashed twice and the fly fell, neatly cut into four parts.

'Superb!' exclaimed the judge.

Finally it was the third samurai's turn. The judge opened another small box and a third fly buzzed out. The samurai's sword flashed through the air – and the fly continued to buzz away. The third samurai put up his sword with a small, satisfied smile on his face.

'But the fly still lives,' observed the judge.

'True,' replied the samurai, ' But he will never reproduce again!'

A young Chinese couple are relaxing in bed after having made love. The husband says to his wife, 'Honey, you know what I could really go for right now is some sixty-nine. How about it?'

His wife looks at him and says, 'You mean you expect me to get out of bed and fry you up some rice and broccoli? No way!'

A Chinese scholar was lecturing when all the lights in the auditorium suddenly went out. He asked members of the audience to raise their hands. As soon as they had all complied, the lights went on again. 'Prove wisdom of old Chinese saying,' he announced. '"Many hands make light work."'

The three worst Chinese torture tests

A traveller in the Chinese wilderness became hopelessly lost. It had been nearly three weeks since he had eaten anything other than what he could forage, and he had been reduced to sleeping in caves and under trees.

One afternoon he happened upon an old mansion set in deep woods. It had vines covering most of it, and the traveller could not see any other buildings in the area. Yet the smoke from the chimney indicated that someone was at home. Taking his courage in both hands, he approached the house and knocked on the door, which was opened by an ancient Chinese with a wispy white beard that reached almost to the ground. The old man squinted myopically at the stranger and said, 'What do you want?'

'I have been lost for the past three weeks,' he replied, 'and haven't eaten or slept properly in all that time. I would be most grateful if you could provide me with a simple meal and let me sleep in your house for tonight.'

The old Chinese considered this for a moment, then said, 'I'll let you come in on one condition: you cannot mess around' – he used the dialect word, *hankipan kee* – 'with my granddaughter'.

The traveller, exhausted and close to starving, readily agreed, saying, 'I promise I won't cause you any trouble. I'll be on my way tomorrow morning, if you will kindly give me directions to the nearest town.'

To this the old man countered, 'All right, but if I do catch you, then I shall give you the three worst Chinese torture tests ever known to man.'

'All right, fine – I agree,' the traveller said as he entered the old house. Besides, he thought to himself, what kind of woman would live out here in the wilderness all her life?

Well, that night, when, after showering, the traveller came down to eat, he saw at once how beautiful the old man's granddaughter was. She was an absolute pearl, and while he had only been lost for three weeks, he had been many, many months without companionship. As for the girl, in all her life the only men she had seen, apart from her grandfather, had been the occasional monk and – well, neither of them could keep their eyes off each other throughout the meal.

That night, when he judged that the old Chinese would be asleep, the traveller crept into the girl's bedroom and, within minutes, into her bed and her arms. They had quite a time but, mindful of the old man's warning, tried to keep the noise to a minimum. Then, sated, the traveller crept back to his room in the early hours, thinking to himself, 'Any three torture tests would be worth it after that experience.'

When morning came, however, he awoke to find a heavy weight on his chest. Opening his eyes, he saw that he was lying beneath a huge rock. Fastened to it was a hand-written sign that read, 'First Chinese torture test: 100-pound rock on your chest.'

'What a lame torture test,' the traveller thought to himself. He struggled up, walked over to the window, opened the shutter and threw the rock out. As he did so, he noticed that on the other side of the rock was another sign that read, 'Second worst Chinese torture test: rock tied to right testicle.'

The traveller, realizing the rock had fallen too far to be grabbed, leapt after it. Hanging outside the window was a third sign, on which he read, as he fell, 'Third worst Chinese torture test: left testicle tied to bedpost.'

Ireland

The trouble with Ireland is that it's a country full of genius, but with absolutely no talent.
Hugh Leonard

The Irish are a fair people – they never speak
well of one another.

Samuel Johnson

Italy, at least, has two things to balance its
miserable poverty and mismanagement: a lively
intellectual movement and a good climate.
Ireland is Italy without these two . . .
. . . Ireland has the honour of being the only
country which never persecuted Jews – because
she never let them in.

James Joyce

I showed my appreciation of my native land in
the usual Irish way by getting out as soon as I
possibly could . . .
  (*so did Joyce, as it happens*)
. . . Put an Irishman on the spit, and you can
always get another Irishman to turn him.

George Bernard Shaw

Where would the Irish be without someone to be
Irish at?

Elizabeth Bowen, The House in Paris

No man is thoroughly miserable unless he is
condemned to live in Ireland.

Jonathan Swift

The Irish climate is wonderful, but the weather
ruins it.

Tony Butler

I never met anyone in Ireland who understands
the Irish question, except one Englishman who
had only been there a week.

Sir Keith Fraser

When I die I want to decompose in a barrel of
porter and have it served in all the pubs in
Dublin. I wonder would they all know it was
me? . . .

. . . To marry the Irish is to look for poverty.

J.P. Donleavy

If it was raining soup, the Irish would be out
with forks.

Brendan Behan

The Irish behave exactly as they have been
portrayed as behaving for years. Charming, soft-
voiced, quarrelsome, priest-ridden, feckless and
happily devoid of the slightest integrity in our
stodgy English sense of the word.

Noël Coward, Diary

If, in the eyes of an Irishman, there is anyone
being more ridiculous than an Englishman, it is
an Englishman who loves Ireland.

André Maurois, Ariel

'You disapprove of the Swedes?'
'Yes, sir.'
'Why?'
'Their heads are too square, sir.'

'And you disapprove of the Irish?'
'Yes, sir.'
'Why?'
'Because they are Irish, sir.'

              P.G. Wodehouse, The Small Bachelor

Criticism of the ENGLISH – Our Weather, Our Food . . .

But, dammit, there do seem to be rather a lot of people who don't fully appreciate *us* (and some are Brits too!) . . .

The Englishman who visits Mount Etna will carry his tea-kettle to the top.

        Ralph Waldo Emerson, English Traits

The most dangerous thing in the world is to make a friend of an Englishman, because he'll come sleep in your closet rather than spend ten shillings on a hotel.

        Truman Capote

The English think incompetence is the same thing as sincerity.

        Quentin Crisp

Continental people have sex lives. The English have hot-water bottles.

George Mikes, How To Be An Alien

The English have sex on the brain – which is a frightfully uncomfortable place to have it.

Malcolm Muggeridge

There is such a thing as too much couth.

S.J. Perelman

Unmitigated noodles.

Kaiser Wilhelm II of Germany, on the English. (It was also the Kaiser who referred to the British Expeditionary Force that faced his invading army in Belgium in August 1914 as 'General French's contemptible little army' – hence the nickname 'Old Contemptibles', which the survivors of the original BEF took for themselves.

Funny, that – on 11 November 1918, Germany surrendered, ending the First World War. A few days later the Kaiser fled to exile in Holland, where he died in 1941 while that country was under German occupation)

A demon took a monkey to wife – the result, by the grace of God, was the English.

Indian saying

The English think soap is civilization.

Heinrich von Treitschke

Britain is the only country in the world where being 'too clever by half' is an insult.

A.A. Gill

The English have no exalted sentiment. They can all be bought . . .
. . . England is a nation of shopkeepers.

Napoleon Bonaparte

The English instinctively admire any man who has no talent and is modest about it.

James Agate

What a pity it is that we have no amusements in England but vice and religion.

Sydney Smith (1771-1845)

England: a good land and a bad people.

Traditional French saying

An Englishman will burn his bed to catch a flea.

Traditional Turkish proverb

The perfidious, haughty, savage, disdainful, stupid, slothful, inhospitable, inhuman English.

Julius Caesar Scaliger (1540-1609)

You must look out in England that you are not cheated by the charioteers.

Marcus Tullius Cicero (106-43 BC)

It is related of an Englishman that he hanged
himself to avoid the daily task of dressing and
undressing.

Johann Wolfgang von Goethe (1749-1832)

A pirate spreading misery and ruin over the face
of the Earth.

Thomas Jefferson (1743-1826), of Britain

The English are, I think, the most obtuse and
barbarous people in the world.

Stendhal (Marie Henri Beyle; 1783-1842)

The two sides of industry [i.e. management and
workforce] have traditionally always regarded
each other in Britain with the greatest possible
loathing, mistrust and contempt. They are both
absolutely right.

Auberon Waugh on British labour relations

In all the four corners of the earth, one of these

three names is given to him who steals from his
neighbour – brigand, robber or Englishman.

Les Triades des Anglais, *1572*

I know why the sun never sets on the British
Empire: God wouldn't trust an Englishman in
the dark.

Duncan Spaeth (1868-1954)

They are naturally lazy, and spend half their
time in taking tobacco.

Samuel de Sorbière (1615-1670), of the English

The English people on the whole are surely the
nicest people in the world, and everyone makes
everything so easy for everybody else, that there
is almost nothing to resist at all.

D.H. Lawrence, Dull London *(there it is –
having a go at niceness again . . .)*

The Devil take these people and their language!
They take a dozen monosyllabic words in their
jaws, chew them, crunch them and spit them out

again, and call that speaking. Fortunately they are by nature fairly silent, and although they gaze at us open-mouthed, they spare us long conversations . . .

. . . These people have no ear, either for rhythm or music, and their unnatural passion for pianoforte playing and singing is thus all the more repulsive. There is nothing on earth more terrible than English music, except English painting . . .

. . . Silence – a conversation with an Englishman.

Heinrich Heine

The English take their pleasures sadly, after the fashion of their country.

Maximilien de Béthune, Duc de Sully
(interestingly, the English surname Bethune is
pronounced 'Beaten')

A family with the wrong members in control – that, perhaps, is as near as one can come to describing England in a phrase.

George Orwell, The Lion and the Unicorn, 'The
Ruling Class'

Mortar fire is to be preferred, of course, to British sports fans.

P.J. O'Rourke, Holidays in Hell

To learn English you must begin by thrusting the jaw forward, almost clenching the teeth, and practically immobilizing the lips. In this way the English produce the series of unpleasant little mews of which their language consists.

José Ortega y Gasset (1883-1955)

All Englishmen talk as if they've got a bushel of plums stuck in their throats, and then after swallowing them get constipated from the pits.

W.C. Fields (1879-1946)

Only Englishmen and dogs walk in the sun.
Italian saying (perhaps it was from this that Noël Coward gained the inspiration for his famous song, 'Mad Dogs and Englishmen Go Out in the Midday Sun')

British towns are like a deck of cards that have
been shuffled and endlessly redealt – same cards,
different order.

Bill Bryson, Notes from a Small Island

An Englishman, even if he is alone, forms an
orderly queue of one.

George Mikes

But Lord! To see the absurd nature of
Englishmen, that cannot forbear laughing and
jeering at everything that looks strange.

Samuel Pepys, Diary

The national sport of England is obstacle racing.
People fill their rooms with useless and
cumbersome furniture, and spend the rest of
their lives in trying to dodge it.

Herbert Beerbohm Tree

It is impossible for an Englishman to open his mouth without making some other Englishman hate or despise him.

George Bernard Shaw, Pygmalion (*Alan Jay Lerner's version of this play, the musical* My Fair Lady, *has the lines: 'An Englishman's way of speaking absolutely classifies him. The moment he talks he makes some other Englishman despise him.'*)

Pass a law to give every single whingeing bloody Pommie his fare home to England. Back to the smoke and the sun shining ten days a year and shit in the streets. Yer can have it.

Thomas Keneally, The Chant of Jimmie Blacksmith

England is a museum of style.

Tom Wolfe, Friends

If an Englishman gets run down by a truck he apologizes to the truck.

Jackie Mason, Independent, *1990*

We really like dowdiness in England. It's absolutely incurable in us, I believe.

Peter Shaffer, Whom Do I Have the Honour of Addressing?, 1990

Even crushed against his brother in the Tube, the average Englishman pretends desperately that he is alone.

Germaine Greer, The Female Eunuch

The English may not like music, but they absolutely love the noise it makes.

Sir Thomas Beecham, New York Herald Tribune, *1961*

Contrary to popular belief, English women do not wear tweed nightgowns.

Hermione Gingold, Saturday Review, *1955*

You never find an Englishman among the underdogs – except in England, of course.

Evelyn Waugh, The Loved One

The old English belief that if a thing is
unpleasant it is automatically good for you.
Osbert Lancaster, Homes Sweet Homes

This Englishwoman is so refined
She has no bosom and no behind.
Stevie Smith, 'This Englishwoman'

He is a typical Englishman, always dull and
usually violent.
Oscar Wilde, An Ideal Husband

Englishmen never will be slaves: they are free to
do whatever the Government and public opinion
allow them to do . . .

. . . An Englishman thinks he is moral when he
is only uncomfortable.
George Bernard Shaw, Man and Superman

In England it is very dangerous to have a sense of humour.

E. V. Lucas, 365 Days and One More

The British tourist is always happy abroad as long as the natives are waiters.

Robert Morley

I like the English. They have the most rigid code of immorality in the world.

Malcolm Bradbury

There are three things to beware of: the hoof of a horse, the horn of a bull, and the smile of an Englishman.

Seamus MacManus

Those comfortably padded lunatic asylums which are known, euphemistically, as the stately homes of England.

Virginia Woolf

The English find ill health not only interesting but respectable, and often experience death in the effort to avoid a fuss.

Pamela Frankau

When an Englishman is totally incapable of doing any work whatsoever, he describes himself on his income-tax form as a 'gentleman'.

Robert Lynd

We do not regard Englishmen as foreigners. We look on them only as rather mad Norwegians.

Harlvard Lange

Thirty millions, mostly fools.
  Thomas Carlyle, *when asked about the population of England*

The English will never forgive a man for being clever.

Lord Hailsham

One of the freedoms of the English is the freedom from culture.

Lord Goodman

If somebody tells you an obviously untrue story, on the Continent you would remark 'You are a liar, sir, and a rather dirty one at that.' In England you just say 'Oh, is that so?' Or 'That's rather an unusual story, isn't it?'

George Mikes, How to Be An Alien

A selection of expressions officially sanctioned by the East German Communist government in the early 1950s for use in describing Britain:

Paralytic sycophants
Effete betrayers of humanity
Carrion-eating servile imitators
Arch-cowards and collaborators
Gang of women-murderers
Degenerate rabble
Parasitic traditionalists
Playboy soldiers
Conceited dandies

People have also been known to criticize our weather . . .

It is cowardly to commit suicide. The English often kill themselves – it is a malady caused by the humid climate.

Napoleon Bonaparte

The way to endure summer in England is to have it framed and glazed in a comfortable room.
Horace Walpole (1717-97)

> The English winter – ending in July,
> To recommence in August.
> *Lord Byron*, Don Juan

I did a picture in England one winter and it was so cold I almost got married.

Shelley Winters

The climate of England has been the world's
most powerful colonizing impulse.

Russell Green

I don't desire to change anything in England
except the weather.

Oscar Wilde

No warmth, no cheerfulness, no healthful
ease,
No comfortable feel in any member –
No shade, no shine, no butterflies, no bees,
No fruits, no flowers, no leaves, no birds, –
November!

Thomas Hood, 'No!', 1844

. . . and even to be rude about our food

English cuisine is generally so threadbare that for
years there has been a gentleman's agreement in
the civilized world to allow the Brits pre-
eminence in the matter of tea – which, after all,

comes down to little more than the ability to boil water.

Wilfrid Sheed

England has forty-two religions and only two sauces.

Voltaire

Go back, you dissolute English. Drink your beer and eat your pickled beef.

La Repentance des Anglais et des Espagnols, c. 1522

The average cooking in the average hotel for the average Englishman explains to a large extent the English bleakness and taciturnity. Nobody can beam and warble while chewing pressed beef smeared with diabolical mustard. Nobody can exult aloud while ungluing from his teeth a quivering tapioca pudding.

Karel Capek (1890-1938)

The English, who eat their meat red and bloody,
show the savagery that goes with such food.

J. de la Mettrie (1709-51)

Belching at table, and in all companies
whatsoever, is a thing which the English no more
scruple than they do coughing and sneezing.

H. Misson de Valbourg (1656-1723)

On the Continent people have good food; in
England people have good table manners.

George Mikes

The English can be explained by their Anglo-
Saxon heritage and the influence of the
Methodists. But I prefer to explain them in terms
of tea, roast beef and rain. A people is first what
it eats, drinks and gets pelted with.

Pierre Daninos, Major Thompson and I

What two ideas are more inseparable than Beer
and Britannia?

Sydney Smith

They have a lot of trouble with pronunciation,
because they can't move their jaw muscles,
because of malnutrition caused by wisely
refusing to eat English food.

Dave Barry, Dave Barry Talks Back

Postscript

I wanted to end with something that encapsulates this country, its qualities, its history, traditions and way of life, and everything that we stand to lose if we wetly succumb to EC bureaucracy and the mad notion of a 'United States of Europe'. I can think of nothing better than Shakespeare's lines from *Richard II*:

> This royal throne of kings, this sceptered isle,
> This earth of majesty, this seat of Mars,
> This other Eden, demi-paradise,
> This fortress built by Nature for herself
> Against infection and the hand of war,
> This happy breed of men, this little world,
> This precious stone set in the silver sea,
> Which serves it in the office of a wall,
> Or as a moat defensive to a house,
> Against the envy of less happier lands,
> This blessèd plot, this earth, this realm, this England . . .

William Shakespeare, Richard II

Then a terrible thought struck me. The text of the Lord's Prayer runs to sixty-five words. The Declaration of Independence occupies a single sheet of parchment. These are two of the most important documents in human history. By contrast, a late-1980s EC directive on duck eggs ran to more than 22,000 words.

Against Brussels, therefore, can also be levelled the charge that it murders trees in significant numbers (since each Saturday edition of the *New York Times* is said to consume some fifty acres of Canadian forest, imagine how much forestry civil servants in Brussels must get through). I would like to leave you, therefore, with a vision of what will happen when EC bureaucrats and committees finally get their teeth into standardizing and making politically correct the world's literature throughout the member states. Here, then, is the same speech as we may yet live to see it rewritten:

EC Directive No. 77410/Shak., W./*Ric. II*/Rewrite (PC)

This non-elitist site or location for a democratically elected titular head of state, this island metaphorically possessed of that head of state's emblem of office,

This symbolical soil of non-autocratic power and splendour, this home of a pan-European quick-reaction force (deployed only as a measure of last resort after due consultation among member states),

This place somewhat akin to a religio-mythical garden, approximately equivalent to one-half of an idealized conception of a region or state of supreme bliss,

This defensive position established, metaphorically speaking, by an anthropomorphized conception of the natural world

Against the infectious or contagious spread of human and animal disorders, as also against aggressive acts by other states,

This good-humoured genus of persons regardless of gender, age, race, colour, physical ability or sexual orientation, this microcosm (relatively speaking),

This valuable jewel or gem 'set' (to use a literary conceit) in a silver-coloured sea-type environment,

Which acts like a wall or other protective or defensive structure,

Or like a deep, wide ditch, usually filled with water, surrounding a house, castle etc.,

Against such misguided actions, prompted by resentment, as might be instigated by the governments of states arguably lacking some of this country's advantages,

This – for those adhering to a formal religious belief or other accepted type of faith – consecrated, revered or fortunate area (usually small) of land; this soil, dry land or ground; this province or domain of the democratically elected titular head of state; this United Kingdom of Great Britain and Northern Ireland (including such islands and other territories as may fall within the legal definition of the title 'United Kingdom') . . .